People who love to eat are always the best people.
— Julia CHILD

BON

appétit !

the delicious life
of Julia CHILD

by

jessie HARTLAND

schwartz & wade books
★ new york ★

This one's for my son, Sam, catcher and cooker of FISH.

Thanks to my great friend Isabelle Dervaux for help with French translations on the endpapers. More *merci beaucoup*s to Etienne Perrot and Coline Drevo for further help. Thanks to my agent, Brenda Bowen, for finding the perfect home for the book. So clever! And to my wonderful editors, Anne and Lee. Just the right amount of poking and prodding. And lastly, thanks to my mom, Dottie Hill Hartland, for fabricating for Xmas 1965 the brilliant French café dollhouse (complete with tiny food and menus in French!), which got me started on France, cooking, and Julia Child.

—J.H.

The galantine recipe in this book was adapted from *The French Chef Cookbook* by Julia Child, copyright © 1968 by Julia Child. Used by permission of Alfred A. Knopf, a division of Random House, Inc.

Copyright © 2012 by Jessie Hartland

All rights reserved. Published in the United States by Schwartz & Wade Books, an imprint of Random House Children's Books, a division of Random House, Inc., New York.

Schwartz & Wade Books and the colophon are trademarks of Random House, Inc.

Visit us on the Web! randomhouse.com/kids

Educators and librarians, for a variety of teaching tools, visit us at randomhouse.com/teachers

Library of Congress Cataloging-in-Publication Data
Hartland, Jessie.
Bon appetit! : the delicious life of Julia Child / Jessie Hartland. —1st ed.
p. cm.
Summary: A picture book biography of Julia Child, the famous chef—Provided by publisher.

ISBN 978-0-375-86944-0 (trade)
ISBN 978-0-375-96944-7 (glb)
1. Child, Julia—Juvenile literature.
2. Women cooks—United States—Biography—Juvenile literature.
3. Graphic novels. I. Title.
TX649.C47H37 2012
641.5092—dc23
[B]
2011018658

The text in this book was lettered by hand.
The illustrations were rendered in gouache.
MANUFACTURED IN MALAYSIA

10 9 8 7 6 5 4 3 2 1

First Edition

Random House Children's Books supports the First Amendment and celebrates the right to read.

She bubbled over with effervescence, spoke as if she had marbles in her mouth, and gleefully hammed it up in front of the camera.

She wrote a classic French cookbook that still sells oodles of copies.

She joined a SPY mission during World War II...

She created and starred in a pioneering TV show loved by millions.

...and later moved to Paris and learned to cook.

How did a gangly girl from Pasadena do it? This is her story.

Julia McWilliams is born in Pasadena, California, in 1912.

orange tree

She is the oldest of three children.

Julia   John   Dort

ALL are TALL.

Pasadena is a town with orange groves, palm trees, and lovely weather year-round.

Julia plays dangerous games on roller skates. This one is called "hooking."

The prankster also builds tree houses, rides her bike everywhere, and throws mud pies at cars.

PASADENA BUS COMPANY

She is a true tomboy.

CALIFORNIA
PASADENA
Los Angeles

The McWilliams family is wealthy. They even have their own cook.

The cook serves mostly meat and potatoes.

Julia's mom only makes dinner on cook's night off and can prepare exactly three dishes:

biscuits

codfish balls

and Welsh rabbit

What the heck is Welsh rabbit?

It's a mix of beer cheese mustard that is cooked together and served over toast.

Nothing to do with bunnies.

whew.

Julia loves to eat! She is certainly

NOT one of those tedious picky eaters. You know the type.

Julia's unusual HEIGHT makes dancing class awkward—

for the 1920s, anyway.

But it comes in handy for basketball.

She is team captain.

What is her favorite after-school snack?

A jelly doughnut!

Julia is sent to the finest private schools and gets a great education, but she really doesn't take school all that seriously.

High school French class is a disaster.

Je ne comprends pas.

Très mal!

(She will make up for this later.)

Just like her mom, she goes to Smith, an all-women's college in the East.

She is a hearty partier and still a prankster. She is famous for painting a toilet seat in her dormitory RED.

FRENCH

SMITH

8

Katherine Branson School

California   U.S.A.   Massachusetts

World War II begins. For the first time, Women are asked to join the armed forces.

1942

Julia moves to Washington, D.C., and tries to enlist, but she is considered TOO TALL.

There is a new government agency, the Office of Strategic Services, and Julia gets a job with them.

She is shipped off to an island called Ceylon (now Sri Lanka).

The OSS is a spy agency. Julia likes to joke that OSS stands for "Oh So Secret."

One of her projects is to help develop a shark repellant to keep curious sharks away from underwater explosives meant to destroy enemy ships.

Kandy CEYLON Kandy

Julia's main job is organizing classified papers. She really likes her coworkers... especially PAUL CHILD, who is 10 years older and far more sophisticated than she is.

APAN

And what did YOU do before the OSS, Paul?

I was a teacher. I carved wood and made stained-glass windows. After that, I was a painter and photographer, and I lived in Paris.

Coincidentally, they both get transferred to China, where they like to try new restaurants together.

They have fish-head soup, ox tongue with tripe, snails, frogs, pig intestine, jellyfish with fish belly, pigs' ears with fish roe...

MENU

Let's order it all! I'm hungry!

When the war ends, they both move back to the United States.

♥ ♥ They fall in love. ♥ ♥

Kunming CHINA Kunming

Paul is a quiet, serious, cultured guy; Julia, a big friendly California gal. They complement each other.

They move to a small house in Georgetown, a neighborhood in Washington, D.C.

Julia and Paul marry in 1946. (Julia is 34.) (Paul is 44.)

In the evenings she tries to cook.

Paul and his twin brother were raised by a single, artistic mom.

Though it is unusual for the time, Paul supports the idea that a woman can have a career outside the home.

Julia works as a file clerk.

Paul works for a branch of the State Department, a federal agency. He plans and mounts exhibitions that aim to show the world what American art and culture look like.

move it up a bit.

Washington, D.C.   U.S.A.   Washington, D.C.

They arrive in France on a rainy day in November 1948.

On the way to Paris, they stop for lunch in Rouen.

* Me too!

Le Havre FRANCE Le Havre

Julia and Paul find an apartment at 81 rue de l'Université, on the Left Bank of the Seine River.

They call their place Roo de Loo.

In his spare time, Paul likes to draw and take photos.

This is Julia's cat, Minette.

Fête de la Musique

ART

JAZZ

81

Julia still wants a career and tries hatmaking. But it is not to be.

What does Julia really like to do? EAT!

Someone suggests she take cooking classes. She likes the idea and enrolls at the famous Cordon Bleu cooking school.

LE CORDON BLEU

At first she is put into a beginners' class.

And now we all know how to make toast!

But after 2 days she transfers to a professional class.

Her classmates are 11 ex-WWII soldiers training to be restaurant chefs.

They learn
how to make

...Soups

Sauces

MILK

OiL

like béchamel

TEACHER

like oignon

...main courses

CHEF
Bugnard

...and desserts

like

like

BURGUNDY WINE

flour

BRANDY

boeuf Bourguignon

crêpes Suzette.

17 Mold the chicken back to its original shape and sew up with a trussing needle.

18 Wrap muslin around it and tie the ends with string.

19 Lay the chicken in a roaster.

20 Add 3 onions, 2 carrots, and 3 celery stalks.

21 Season with a bay leaf, 2 t thyme, and 8 parsley sprigs.

22 Add the chicken carcass bones and, if you wish, some veal knuckles and calves' feet.

23 Fill pan to 1½" with chicken broth. Add a glass of white wine and 2 T of old brandy.

24 Cover the whole thing with a piece of buttered parchment paper. Cook over a high flame and bring to a simmer.

25 Turn down the heat and simmer slowly for 3 hours. Remove from the heat.

26 After an hour, lift the galantine out of the pan and place it on a platter.

27 Cover with a lid and an 8-lb weight.

28 When the galantine has cooled, remove the string.

29 Remove the muslin, gently press out any juices, and dry the outside with a cloth.

30 Strain the jelly that has accumulated on the platter through a sieve, remove the fat, clarify it, and then brush it on. This is called aspic.

31 Put the galantine on a serving plate and decorate it with pimiento, blanched pistachios, pickled udder, blanched leeks, truffles, and pickled tongue.

32 Finally, glaze with 2 more coats of aspic.

Pigs and dogs are trained to sniff them out. A black truffle this size can cost about $40.

actual size

Here's a little something I just whipped up!
Voilà!!!
La pièce de résistance!!!

Julia goes to lots of parties,

and at one she meets a French-woman named Simone Beck, nicknamed Simca.

S
I
M
C
A

She also loves to cook, read about food, and talk about food.

Larousse Gastro-nomique

Simca and her friend Louisette Bertholle

are trying to write a FRENCH cookbook for Americans, without much success.

Another rejection! Tant pis! *

Zut alors! **

* Too bad! ** Darn it!

One day Julia reads a magazine article by an American complaining about the lack of good kitchen knives in the United States.

HARPER'S magazine

In appreciation, she sends the writer two small French steel knives.

Air mail
DeVoto
Cambridge, mass.
U.S.A.

This is a pivotal moment.

A correspondence is started with the writer's wife, AVIS DeVOTO.

A new pen pal!

Avis Julia AVIS Julia! avis Julia AVIS Julia VIS Julia AVIS

In 1951 Julia graduates from the Cordon Bleu.

le cordon bleu
DIPLOME
Mme CHILD 1951

Julia and her friends Simca and Louisette start a cooking school of their own.

Ecole Des 3 Gourmandes

It's called *

Paul designs the logo.

The classes are given in Julia's Kitchen.

The students are mostly American women found through the embassy.

* "The school of the 3 Hearty Eaters."

The fish market is right at Julia's door. She loves the famous mediterranean fish stew called bouillabaisse and wants to know how to make it.
BONJOUR!! I'm looking for the TRUE, classic bouillabaisse ** recipe.
NO lobster!
NO Saffron!
It MUST have butter.
It MUST have mussels!
O BUTTER!
huîtres
praires
clavisses
moules
Pas de moules! *
Bouillabaisse MUST have saffron!
Never put in eels.
Always—lobster!
POISSONS
homards
MARSEILLE
* NO mussels!
** say "boo-ya-BESS"

Paul next gets transferred to Plittersdorf, Germany.

It's hard to pick up and move every few years so correspondence with friends is even more important!

Julia sends Avis some shallots.

Avis sends Julia authentic American ingredients (important for working out the recipes).

Julia and Simca exchange 60 pages of letters about whether preserved goose is essential to a French stew called a cassoulet.

(Louisette has become less involved in the cookbook.)

*I'm hungry!

Plittersdorf GERMANY Plittersdorf

Julia and Simca get a letter from Boston.
Rejected!
They want a shorter, simpler book. More shortcuts. Like using mixes and canned things...
HM
Mon Dieu. Quelle horreur!* That's not French!
* my God. How appalling!
I don't like the shortcut idea either. But we can still do a simpler book. Can't we?
Yes. Let's get to work.
AIR FRANCE
bye!
au revoir!
Paul is next transferred to Oslo, Norway, for 2 years. Julia works on her skiing, gives some cooking lessons,
and learns some essential Norwegian:
Jeg er sulten!*
*I'm hungry.
NORWAY
SWEDEN
Oslo
EUROPE
Oslo NORWAY Oslo

Julia is working on the FISH RECIPES.
First she might try 10 existing recipes for one dish.
Hmmm... I think I can improve on that.
Poissons
Seafood
FISH
1
Voilà! A new (and improved) recipe!
2
Then she might rework it... and make it 8 times!
3
Tweak it.
mmm... mussels!
Cook it again.
4
Then she might develop a new technique.
5
Moules 7
And troubleshoot. How might cooks make mistakes?
Hmmm.... mussels.
6
more detailed instructions.
Mussels again?
Paul is the guinea pig.
7
Fine-tune it, cook it 6 more times.
Julia is a perfectionist.
8
The final result? An original recipe! And it's foolproof.
9

Whew. Finally.

Julia ships off a NEW version of the cookbook. It's 750 pages and has everything, soup to nuts.

AIR MAIL

But their publisher still thinks the book is too long and involved.

Simca, they want MORE changes!

It is very sad.

Then Julia's friend Avis has an idea. She knows another publisher who might like the book.

J u d i t h

J o n e s.

And one day in 1959 the manuscript lands on the desk of a young editor in New York named

Judith Jones is known for having discovered a now-famous Dutch book and publishing it in America.

ANNE FRANK DIARY
HET Achterhuis

ACCEPT

REJECT

I've GOT to make an offer on this one.

COOKBOOKS

TRAV

Judith herself loves to cook. And she lived in France for 3 years.

Iceland
E-Z BRIT MEALS
FOOD OF CANADA
ZANZIBAR
NORTH CANADA COOKIN'
1-2-3 OF CONGO COOKING
Alaskan MEALS
LATVIAN
TIBET
SPAIN
ISH
IRAN
Belgian
BRONX Eats
Nigerian Cuisine
CHINA
EGYPT COOKING
CHILI from Chile

Hmmm, No French cookbooks?

She knows there is no really good French cookbook in America.

Judith spends months

FRENCH RECIPES for AMERICAN COOKS

This boeuf Bourguignon * is a winner. This cookbook is a winner!

I've GOT to make an offer on this one!

trying out many of the recipes.

* Beef stew with Burgundy wine.

And she does.
... and Julia? The title? It's awful. We need a new one.
Julia Knows that getting the title of the book just right is important.
She asks people to help and offers a prize to the winner-
foie gras en bloc truffé*
What the heck is that?
* Fattened goose liver molded in a block with truffles.
French Cooking for the American Supermarket?
NO.
LOVE and French Cooking?
NO.
FOOD, France, Fun
NO.
French Magician in the Kitchen?
The Passionate French Cook?
NO, NO.
French Kitchen Pleasure?
Non
French Food, at Last?
No
Mastering the Art of French Cooking?
Oui, oui, OUI! You get the prize, Judith.

That same year, when Paul retires from the State Department, he and Julia move to Cambridge, just outside Boston.

Paul grew up in Boston, and they already have friends in the area. They buy a house with a nice big kitchen.

And they sign copies in bookstores.

HERE at 3pm
Julia Child
Simone Beck
"Mastering the Art of French Cooking"

Julia and Simca work hard to promote the new book—

Practice flipping with beans!

NEW FRENCH COOKBOOK!

OMELET demo at 12

They give demonstrations in department stores.

They are interviewed on the radio...

ON THE AIR

It took 10 years.

C'est vrai, 10 ans. *

* It's true, 10 year

Cambridge, mass. U.S.A Cambridge, mass.

The French Chef

1. So many people love the demo that Boston public TV station WGBH offers Julia her own cooking show.

2. I'd like to call it The French Chef. It's short and to-the-point!

3. Even people who don't like to cook watch the show and love it!

4. The TV show does not pay particularly well, but it is good publicity for the cookbooks.

5. Julia Child presents the chicken sisters! Miss Broiler! Miss Fryer! miss Roaster! Miss Caponette! Miss Stewer! And old Madame Hen!

The Chicken Show!

6. And Julia's advice should something fall on the floor?

You can always pick it up!

If you are alone in the kitchen, whoooooo is going to see?

7. The shows are not live, but — to save money — they are all shot in "one take" (no editing), which is tricky.

Oh, nuts! I burned the sauce.
I'm Julia Child. Bon appétit!*
Don't apologize for your cooking mistakes. It is what it is.
Ecole Des 3 Gourmandes
*She ends each show saying this.

Julia Child is now famous! Her hard work has brought her great success, and this allows her and Paul to build a house in Provence, in the South of France.

farine   sucre   riz

mastering the Art 2

mastering the Art of French cooking
The French Chef cookbook
Julia C. and more company
Baking with Julia

cooking with master chefs

Julia Child + Company

LAIT

Julia Child's menu cookbook
The WAY to cook

Julia's kitchen wisdom

Pomme

pomme de terre

ananas

gâteau

tarte

sel

Pamplemousse

Poisson

Citron

beurre

verre

assiette

vin   eau

fourchette

serviette

poubelle

She goes on to write many more books.

petites cuillères

couteaux

gamelle

poivre

champignons

ail

fromage

oeuf

Because she is so tall, she has the kitchen counters custom-built so that they are higher.

souris

chaussures taille 12

NOW YOU can make your own CRÊPES!

Be sure
to ask a
grown-up
to
help
you.

Now crack
3 eggs

you have
flour on
your face!

Jessie's Crêpes

3 eggs — 1 cup of milk — 3/4 cup of flour — a bit of butter

BEAT the eggs with a whisk. ADD the milk and whisk a little more. ADD the flour and beat some more. POUR the mixture through a fine strainer into a 1-quart glass measuring cup. USE a rubber scraper to push it through.

MELT 1T of butter in a frying pan until it is quite hot but not smoking. WHISK the batter a bit, then pour about 1/4 cup into the pan. The heat should be on medium high.

COOK the crêpe for only about 30 seconds, until it has cooked through, then flip it over and cook a little more. It should be *slightly* brown on both sides.

MAKE more crêpes, adding small bits of butter to the pan as you need to. YOU can keep a pile of crêpes warm on a plate by placing a cloth on top.

CRÊPES are delicious with maple syrup and fresh fruit. PUT some powdered sugar on top! THIS recipe serves about 3 people. YOU can multiply the recipe to serve more. A 6-egg batch serves 6, etc. Bon appétit!

Learn
more about...

Steve Hansen//Time Life Pictures/Getty Images

You can see Julia Child's actual kitchen from her house in Cambridge, Massachusetts, at the Smithsonian National Museum of American History in Washington, D.C. You can also see it online at american history.si.edu/juliachild.

If you ever go to Rouen, you too can have *déjeuner** at La Couronne (lacouronne.com.fr), where Julia had her first meal in France. It is the oldest restaurant in the country.

*lunch.

BIBLIOGRAPHY

I read many wonderful books while researching *Bon Appétit: The Delicious Life of Julia Child*.
Here are some of them:

Barr, Nancy Verde. *Backstage with Julia: My Years with Julia Child*. Hoboken, New Jersey: Wiley & Sons, 2007.

Child, Julia. *The French Chef Cookbook*. New York: Knopf, 1968.

———. *Julia Child and More Company*. New York: Knopf, 1979.

Child, Julia, with Alex Prud'homme. *My Life in France*. New York: Knopf, 2006.

Child, Julia, Louisette Bertholle, and Simone Beck. *Mastering the Art of French Cooking*. Vol. 1. New York: Knopf, 1961.

Child, Julia, and Simone Beck. *Mastering the Art of French Cooking*. Vol. 2. New York: Knopf, 1970.

Fitch, Noel Riley. *Appetite for Life*. New York: Random House, 1997.

Reardon, Joan. *As Always, Julia: The Letters of Julia Child and Avis DeVoto*. New York: Houghton Mifflin Harcourt, 2010.

Root, Waverley. *The Food of France*. Rev. ed. New York: Knopf, 1970.

Shapiro, Laura. *Julia Child*. New York: Penguin, 2007.

I also looked at lots of old books of photographs of Paris and France and food in the 1950s and viewed on DVD many episodes of Julia Child's TV show.

Clébert, Jean-Paul; photographs by Patrice Molinard. *Paris que j'aime*. Paris: Editions Sun, 1956.

The French Chef with Julia Child. Discs 1 and 2. WGBH, Boston, 2005.

Montagne, Prosper. *Larousse Gastronomique*. New York: Crown, 1961. Originally published in French by Librairie Larousse, Paris. 6th printing, 1965.

Réné-Jacques. *Paris*. Paris: Bibliothèque des arts, 1967.

Roth, Beulah. *Paris in the Fifties: Photographs by Sanford Roth*. San Francisco: Mercury House, 1988.